Frida Kahlo

Robyn Montana Turner

Little, Brown and Company
Boston   Toronto   London

To my father

ACKNOWLEDGMENTS

I'd like to extend my grateful appreciation to the many individuals who influenced the development of this series and this book, including my editors, Maria Modugno and Hilary M. Breed, for tenaciously seeing this book through to completion; Virginia A. Creeden for gathering permissions for the images from around the world; Suzanne Garrigues; the staff of the Benson Latin American Collection within the Library Systems at the University of Texas at Austin; and Lidia Graciela Agraz, Mary-Anne Martin, Blanca Garduño Pulido, Karen Cordero, Lic. Norma Rojas Delgadllo, Rafael C. Arvea, Herbert Hoover, Salomon Grimberg, and Marilyn Lübetkin for their assistance with photographic permissions. I extend special appreciation to Dr. Rolando Hinojosa-Smith for reviewing the manuscript for cultural authenticity.

First Edition

Quotation on back jacket and page 3 courtesy of *Vogue.* Copyright 1938 (renewed 1966) by Condé Nast Publications, Inc.

Library of Congress Cataloging-in-Publication Data

Turner, Robyn.
    Frida Kahlo / Robyn Montana Turner. — 1st ed.
      p.   cm. — (Portraits of women artists)
    Summary: Celebrates the life and work of the Mexican painter.
    ISBN 0-316-85651-7
    1. Kahlo, Frida — Juvenile literature.   2. Painters — Mexico —
Biography — Juvenile literature. [1. Kahlo, Frida. 2. Artists.]
I. Title. II. Series.
ND259.K33T87   1993
759.972 — dc20
[B]   91-29556

10 9 8 7 6 5 4 3 2 1

SC

Published simultaneously in Canada
by Little, Brown & Company (Canada) Limited

Printed in Hong Kong

The only thing I know is that I paint because I need to, and I paint always whatever passes through my head, without any other consideration.

—Frida Kahlo

Frida Kahlo
(FREE-dah KA-lō) 1907–1954

Just 150 years ago, only a few women in the world had become well known as artists. Since then many women have been recognized for their artwork. Today some very famous artists are women.

Nowadays both boys and girls are encouraged to become great artists. They may attend the best art schools and study together with the finest art teachers. Both men and women have the opportunity to learn to draw, paint, and sculpt images of the human body by studying nude models.

But let's imagine that you could go back in time to the turn of the twentieth century — about a hundred years ago. As a young person growing up in America at that time, you might wonder why women artists in your country have only just recently been allowed to attend the best schools of art. You might question why women artists are not welcome at social gatherings where male artists learn from each other by discussing new ideas about art. You might be surprised to discover that women have just recently been permitted to look at nude models to help them learn how to portray the human figure. And you might be disappointed to learn that most young girls are not encouraged to become great artists.

South of the United States, in Mexico, artistic opportunities for women were not any better. Less than a century ago in Mexico, there lived a young girl who would become well known as an artist anyway. Her name was Frida Kahlo. Today her works of art hang in museums throughout the world.

Nickolas Muray. **Frida Kahlo.** *International Museum of Photography at George Eastman House.*
Today this photograph of Frida hangs over Diego's bed at the Casa Azul.

Frida Kahlo Museum.
Author's photograph. 1991.
The Casa Azul, Frida Kahlo's home, is open today to the public as a museum that houses many of her works of art, furniture, and other memorabilia.

Matilde Calderón de Kahlo and Guillermo Kahlo.
Wedding photograph.
Frida's mother was of Native Mexican and Spanish descent. Her father came to Mexico from Germany.

On the rainy summer morning of July 6, 1907, the third daughter of Matilde Calderón de Kahlo and Guillermo Kahlo came into the world. She was born in Coyoacán, Mexico, then a small village outside Mexico City and now a part of the city. As was the custom in Mexico, the parents gave her a long name — Magdalena Carmen Frida Kahlo y Calderón. For the baby's baptism they would say her Mexican names, Magdalena Carmen, which were from her mother's side of the family. The rest of the time she would be called Frida, which means peace in German, her father's native language.

Three years before Frida's birth, her father had built a beautiful blue house, the Casa Azul, where Frida would live many years of her life. Its heavy stucco walls and flat roof in the shape of a U surrounded a large inner courtyard, where Frida liked to play. From the courtyard she could enter almost any room.

Young Frida's dark hair framed her round face and dimpled chin. Her eyebrows joined above her nose, a trait she inherited from her German grandmother.

As an adult, Kahlo painted a portrait of herself as a two-year-old, *My Grandparents, My Parents, and I (Family Tree)*. Naked and barefoot, she stands firmly planted in the courtyard of the Casa Azul, where she always felt safe and secure. Her sturdy little body serves as the trunk to her family tree. She holds a red ribbon as her bloodline to her grandparents, who float in the clouds above the earth. Kahlo painted the plants and landforms of Mexico beneath her mother's parents, who were of Native Mexican and Spanish descent. She painted the ocean beneath her father's parents, who were of European descent.

To paint the image of her parents, Kahlo studied their wedding photograph. Careful details show every bow and ruffle of her mother's dress and the upturn of her father's mustache. Imagining her own beginnings, Kahlo added the biologically accurate image of a developing fetus in her mother's skirt. The couple floats directly above the family home in Coyoacán. They form a solid backdrop to Frida, who positioned herself at the center of the Casa Azul.

Frida Kahlo. **My Grandparents, My Parents, and I (Family Tree).** (*Mis abuelos, mis padres, y yo.*) *1936. Oil and tempera on metal panel. 12⅛ x 13⅝ inches. Collection, The Museum of Modern Art, New York. Gift of Allan Roos, M.D., and B. Mathieu Roos.* When Kahlo grew up to become an accomplished artist, she painted this image of her childhood from memory and imagination.

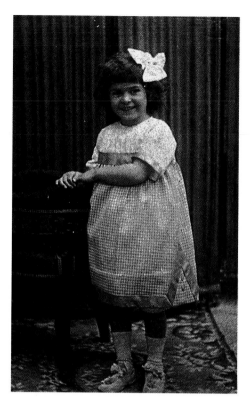

Guillermo Kahlo. **Frida Kahlo at Age Three.** *c. 1910.* Frida's father, who was a professional photographer, took many pictures of her.

Altogether the Kahlos had four daughters: Matilde, Adriana, Frida, and Cristina. Before they entered kindergarten, their mother taught them to sew, embroider, cook, and clean. She took them to church every day and insisted they pray before each meal. Instead of praying, however, Frida and Cristina would peek at each other from across the table, holding back their noisy giggles. The two mischievous girls were supposed to attend catechism classes to prepare for their First Communion in the Catholic church. But oftentimes they would sneak away to a nearby orchard to munch on *capulínes,* a cherrylike fruit.

Free-spirited Frida did not get along very well with her mother, but she was her father's favorite. Frida's zest for life added joy to *don* Guillermo's restless personality. She liked to tease him about his German ways by calling him *Herr Kahlo* (Mister Kahlo). In German he would respond, *"Frida, liebe Frida"* ("Frida, dear Frida"). *Don* Guillermo took pride in telling others that Frida was the most intelligent of his daughters. "She is the most like me," he often remarked.

Just as the fathers of many women artists have encouraged their daughters, *don* Guillermo Kahlo introduced young Frida to artistic ideas and projects. He lent her books from his library and shared his own excitement about nature — plants, animals, shells, stones, birds, and insects. They walked together in nearby parks, where her father dabbled in watercolors while Frida explored the riverbanks. Once at home, they examined under a microscope things she had collected by the river. When Frida was old enough to understand, her father taught her about Mexican archaeology and art and about his own trade — photography.

Frida Kahlo. **Portrait of My Father.** (*Retrato de mi padre.*) *1951. Oil on masonite. 60.5 x 46.5 cm. Museo Frida Kahlo, Mexico City. Reproduction authorized by the National Institute of Fine Arts and Literature.* This portrait of *don* Guillermo reflects his restless, creative, caring personality as Kahlo remembered it.

Many years later, when Kahlo had grown up and her father had died, she painted *Portrait of My Father* as a tribute to him. To help her recall details, Kahlo studied a photograph her father had taken of himself. In Kahlo's painting, *don* Guillermo's round, shiny wide eyes look a lot like the eye, or lens, of his camera. His peaceful gaze seems to cover up his restless feelings. Beneath the portrait, Kahlo wrote about fond memories of her father.

Guillermo Kahlo. **Cristina Kahlo, Isabel Campos, and Frida Kahlo.** 1919.
Frida and her sister Cristina posed for this photograph with their childhood friend Isabel Campos.

Frida Kahlo. **Frida in Coyoacán** (Frida en Coyoacán.) c. 1927.
Watercolor on paper. 16 x 21 cm. Instituto Tlaxcalteca de Cultura, Tlaxcala.
Reproduction authorized by the National Institute of Fine Arts and Literature.
In this watercolor painting, Kahlo positioned herself in the foreground to appear close to the viewer. The trees and buildings are in the middle ground and background.

Among the fond memories, Kahlo recalled the loving care shown by both her parents during her childhood illness. At age six, she was stricken with polio. As a result, the muscles in her right leg stopped growing, and it soon became thinner and a bit shorter than the left.

Helping Frida follow the doctor's advice, *don Guillermo* made sure she exercised through a variety of sports, in which respectable young girls of Mexico rarely participated. Frida, like the boys, played soccer, wrestled, boxed, and became an excellent swimmer.

Even with all of this activity, Frida's right leg remained smaller than her left. Sometimes other children teased her by shouting, *"Frida, pata de palo!"* ("Frida, peg leg!"). She responded with loud and furious curses and hid her leg by wearing three or four socks and a built-up right heel.

During this time Frida created an imaginary friend. To visit her, Frida had only to breathe vapor onto a windowpane in her room. With her finger she would draw a door, through which she would go on an imaginary journey to a place where her friend always waited for her. The friend laughed a lot and danced as if she weighed nothing at all. As she danced with her friend, Frida would explain all of her secret problems. When Frida was ready to return to the real world, she would reenter through the door on the windowpane, then rub it away. She would then run to sit under a cedar tree in the courtyard, where she would laugh aloud about her good feelings and the memory of her imaginary friend.

Because of her bout with polio, Frida entered elementary school later than her friends of the same age, so she told her classmates that she was younger than she really was. And she continued to hide her right leg with long skirts and trousers.

After school, Frida and her girlfriends liked to explore Coyoacán. They played by the river, ran and skipped on the plazas, and knew every street vendor. At neighborhood fairs they ate *quesadillas* (flour tortillas filled with cheese, green chili peppers, and onions), tried out new toys, and talked with the merchants and shoeshine boys.

When Frida turned fifteen, *don* Guillermo enrolled her in the National Preparatory School in Mexico City, an hour's ride from Coyoacán on the trolley. There Frida studied with the best teachers in Mexico. Girls had just recently been admitted to the Preparatoria, and Frida was one of only thirty-five girls among two thousand students. She planned to prepare for medical school.

Frida arrived at the Preparatoria looking like a German schoolgirl in uniform. She dressed in a white blouse with a tie and a blue pleated skirt.

The busy girl filled her school notebooks with sketches. Over her shoulder she carried a knapsack filled with texts, notebooks, drawings, butterflies, dried flowers, and crayons. She soon abandoned her schoolgirl uniform and sometimes wore a man's suit or a dramatic dress that she herself designed. On her own, Frida liked to study art history books that showed paintings by artists throughout the ages. She took composition and drawing classes but thought of art not as a serious pursuit but only as something fun to do in her spare time.

She was much more interested in her eight friends, mostly boys, known as the Cachuchas. They were named for their red caps and known for their bright minds and pranks, which sometimes got them into trouble. Once they even rode a donkey through the hallways of the school!

The Cachuchas liked to meet in the library, where they did their schoolwork, teased each

Guillermo Kahlo. **Frida Kahlo as a Child.** *c. 1917.*

other, and discussed important ideas. They planned ways to change the Mexican government. And they had contests to see who could discover a better book and then who could finish reading it first. Sometimes they acted out what they read. Frida learned so much at school and from the Cachuchas that soon she could read in three languages.

Alejandro (Alex) Gómez Arias was the leader of the Cachuchas. Frida called him her *novio,* or sweetheart. They would always be friends.

On September 17, 1925, when Frida was eighteen, something happened that changed her life forever. She and Alex were traveling from Mexico City to Coyoacán in a brightly painted wooden bus when an electric streetcar smashed into the side of it.

Alex found Frida lying in the street bathed in blood. He took care of her until the ambulance arrived. Many of her bones were broken — spine, collarbone, ribs, pelvis, and right leg. Her right foot was crushed. Her most serious injuries were caused when a handrail from the streetcar went through her lower body. Doctors at the Red Cross Hospital thought Frida would die on the operating table.

But Frida had a strong will to live. After only a month, she returned home, wrapped in splints. Alex and other school friends visited her, but soon they grew tired of traveling to Coyoacán. Frida never resumed her studies.

From her bed, however, with her arms and imagination free, Frida began to paint. Her mother ordered a special lap easel, and her father lent her his oil paints. Frida placed a mirror above her on the canopy to paint her self-portrait.

During the next two years, Frida was able to get up and about, even though her health remained poor. Doctors operated on her again and again. At times she wore plaster casts — even around her torso. Frida would never fully recover from the terrible bus accident. The themes of many of her paintings began to reflect her pain.

Kahlo's painting *The Bus* shows that she somehow kept her sense of humor throughout her misfortune. Four years after the accident, she was able to create this whimsical image of the many varieties of people who ride the rickety Mexican bus together. The plump woman with her straw shopping basket, a worker who wears a tie with his overalls and cap, the barefoot mother figure swaddling a baby in her bright *rebozo*, or shawl, the child who is more interested in the world outside, the businessman with his money bag and a dazed look on his face, a prissy young woman — everyone adds a special story to the picture.

When Frida's strength returned, she showed her paintings to some well-known artists. José Clemente Orozco, who painted murals with Mexican themes, liked them so much that he gave her a hug. Then she took her paintings to the most famous Mexican muralist, Diego Rivera.

Frida Kahlo. **The Bus.** (*El camión.*) *1929. Oil on canvas. 25⅛ x 55½ cm. Collection of Delores Olmedo, Mexico. Reproduction authorized by the National Institute of Fine Arts and Literature.*

Frida Kahlo. **Frida and Diego Rivera.** *(Frida y Diego Rivera.) 1931. Oil on canvas. 39⅜ x 31 inches; 100 x 78.7 cm. San Francisco Museum of Modern Art. Albert M. Bender Collection, Gift of Albert M. Bender. 36.6061.* Frida and Diego were known as the elephant and the dove. She painted this work with popular Mexican colors of the day: blues, greens, lavenders, red-oranges, and browns. The ribbon above gives the date and occasion for the portrait.

Diego set aside his paintbrush and climbed down from high scaffolding to view Frida Kahlo's paintings. The next Sunday, he visited her home in Coyoacán, where he fell in love with her paintings and with her.

On August 21, 1929, Frida and Diego were married. At about this time, Frida immersed herself in traditional Mexican culture. She decorated her and Diego's home with Mexican art and wore Mexican clothing. She especially liked Tehuana dresses, the traditional clothing of the strong and independent women of the Tehuantepec region of southern Mexico. As in *The Bus*, Frida's paintings had also begun to express her feelings as a Mexican. Diego's influence as a master muralist caused Frida to become more serious about her own artistic talent.

In 1931 she painted their wedding portrait, *Frida and Diego Rivera*. Diego appears huge beside Frida, his *niña bonita* (pretty young girl), as he called her. He weighed three hundred pounds and was more than six feet tall. Frida affectionately called Diego her *sapo-rana* (toad-frog) and *mi cuate* (my pal). Their paintings reflect the difference in their body sizes. His works cover entire walls of buildings, while many of hers are the size of this book. Together the famous couple was known as the elephant and the dove.

In Frida's double portrait, Diego grips his palette and brushes while he lightly holds his wife's hand. This was Frida's way of showing that above all else Diego was an artist. His initial on his belt buckle and the outward placement of his large feet show that he felt sure of himself.

Frida was only five feet three inches tall and weighed ninety-eight pounds. With a touch of humor, she painted herself as the famous artist's admiring and dainty wife. Not even one paintbrush

appears in her own hand. Her native clothes — a
colorful *rebozo*, a tiered dress, and necklaces of
Mexican stones — show her cultural heritage.

In November 1930, when Frida was twenty-three, she and Diego left Mexico to visit San Francisco, California, where Diego was to paint several murals. Dressed in her native Mexican clothes, Frida caused excitement on the streets. People stopped to look in amazement. She rode the trolley up and down the steep hills. She practiced her English and visited museums. In Chinatown, a historic part of San Francisco, she looked for silk materials to make into long skirts.

One day Kahlo met a doctor who would become her lifelong medical adviser and friend. Dr. Leo Eloesser was the chief of service at San Francisco General Hospital and a professor of surgery at a nearby university. The short, dark-haired surgeon with eyes that twinkled was loved by all who knew him, including Kahlo.

She liked the way Dr. Eloesser gave of his time and talents to people around the world who needed medical care. And she was amused by his unusual habits. For example, at midnight he often left his office and sailed up the bay to Red Rock Island. When the sun came up he would have breakfast on board, then sail back to the city to take care of his patients. He also played stringed instruments with well-known musicians. In fact, Dr. Eloesser stayed so busy that no one could figure out when he slept.

Portrait of Dr. Leo Eloesser is Kahlo's tribute to this respected surgeon. Posing at his home, he wears a dark suit and a white shirt with a starched high collar. He stands stiffly, resting his arm beside a model of a sailing ship. Kahlo had never seen a sailing ship, so she imagined how one might look. Because the doctor was a patron of the arts, she included on the wall a drawing signed "D. Rivera." In the bottom right corner, where artists usually

Frida Kahlo. **Portrait of Dr. Leo Eloesser.** (*Retrato del Dr. Leo Eloesser.*) *1931. Oil on cardboard. 84 x 60 cm. School of Medicine, University of California, San Francisco.* Kahlo's name was originally spelled Frieda, the German spelling, which is how she signed this painting. She dropped the *e* in the 1930s because she was disturbed by the Nazis' rise to power in her father's homeland.

sign their paintings, Kahlo wrote, "For Dr. Leo
Eloesser with all love, Frieda Kahlo. San Francisco
Cal. 1931."

Diego Rivera and Frida Kahlo. *1933. Acme. UPI/The Bettmann Archive.* Frida and Diego lived in New York City while Diego painted a mural in the Rockefeller Center RCA Building. This photograph was taken the day after Nelson Rockefeller dismissed Diego from the project because he disagreed with the political meaning of Diego's mural.

In 1932 Frida and Diego went to Detroit, where he painted murals of the factory workers who built American automobiles. Shortly after the couple returned home, Frida's mother fell ill and died. *Don Guillermo* was terribly sad. Frida and her sisters cried and wore dark shawls to express their sorrow.

Frida and Diego traveled to New York City in 1933 because Diego had been commissioned to paint murals inside the RCA Building there. Each day Frida climbed the scaffolds carrying Diego's lunch in a basket decorated with flowers and covered by napkins embroidered with love notes showing her adoration for him. This was a Mexican custom taken from women who carried their husbands' lunches to them as they worked in the fields. But Diego was often too involved with his art to eat.

New York did not inspire Kahlo to paint. Instead, she read, took care of the apartment, saw friends, played drawing games, shopped, and crossed the Brooklyn Bridge to see Tarzan films. Occasionally Diego took the time to attend a dinner party with her. At one such party, with artist friends, everyone poured powdered sugar all over the white tablecloth and created a landscape by spilling wine, shaking pepper, and moving things around. People always had great fun with Frida and Diego.

But Kahlo missed Mexico. During the entire eight-month stay in New York, she painted only one picture, *My Dress Hangs There.* Each object in the painting represents something that Kahlo disliked about the United States, or "Gringolandia," as she nicknamed it. The painting is a mockery of New York City, which Kahlo saw as a place where money-hungry businesses and severe poverty existed side by side. Her empty Tehuana dress hangs

in the center of it all, which might mean that Kahlo herself chose to be someplace else.

To poke fun at fancy plumbing and competitive sports in the United States, she painted a toilet and a golden trophy on pedestals. Because she felt that businesses and churches worked too closely together, Kahlo changed the cross in the church window to look like a dollar sign. To show her disgust for false values in the U.S., she included a billboard of a famous Hollywood movie star, Mae West, who to Kahlo represented the worship of glamour and vanity. Flames from burning buildings

Frida Kahlo. **My Dress Hangs There (New York).** *(Mi vestido cuelga allí.) 1933. Oil and collage on masonite. 46 x 50 cm. Hoover Gallery, Estate of Dr. Leo Eloesser.* The Tehuana dress was Kahlo's favorite. It is a regional costume from the Isthmus of Tehuantepec.

Diego Rivera and Frida Kahlo. *Acme. UPI/The Bettmann Archive.*

below threaten the billboard. Kahlo represented the American way of life as she saw it — an overflowing pail of human waste.

The statue of George Washington on the steps of Wall Street's Federal Hall and the Statue of Liberty raising her torch are reminders of the ideals on which the United States was founded. But when Kahlo painted this work, during the Great Depression, many Americans were hungry and jobless, represented by the swarming figures at the bottom of the image. Kahlo despised the American system of earning and distributing money, which she felt let the rich get richer while the poor got poorer. Perhaps she painted the puffing ship in the harbor as a wish that it would take her back to Mexico.

On December 20, 1933, Frida and Diego finally sailed home to Mexico. She was happy to see her friends and family. But her life still had physical and emotional pain that seemed impossible to overcome. More than ten years after the bus accident, she had not completely recovered. Many operations had failed to straighten her spine and mend her right foot. And she became even sadder because at about this time it became clear that she would be unable to have children.

Frida once said that she suffered two bad accidents in her life — one was the streetcar collision, and the other was Diego. At times he was difficult to be married to. It was said that Diego was susceptible to love like a weather vane, meaning that he was easily attracted to a variety of women. In addition, his passion for his art required a great deal of time and attention. He needed to paint as much as he needed to eat and sleep. Some said the marriage between Frida and Diego was a union of lions. But throughout their long and stormy relationship, they always loved and needed each other.

For several years, Frida and Diego lived in San Angel, Mexico. Their home there was built so they could each have a studio and plenty of privacy. Eventually they moved back into the Casa Azul.

Frida Kahlo Museum. **Frida Kahlo's Studio.** *Coyoacán, Mexico, D.F.*
Kahlo loved to work in her studio in the Casa Azul.

In 1937 the Casa Azul received two world-famous guests, Leon and Natalia Trotsky. Diego and Frida, who had joined the Mexican section of the Communist Party, welcomed these Russians. The Trotskys had been thrown out of their homeland because of political disagreements with the government. During Leon Trotsky's two-year stay at the Casa Azul, he and Frida became close friends. For his birthday, she painted *Self-Portrait Dedicated to Leon Trotsky.*

In this portrait, Kahlo is dressed in Spanish Colonial clothing, a more formal style than her Tehuana dresses. She stands poised in a stately position between two evenly spaced curtains. In this way, Kahlo gave symmetrical balance to the painting. Her hands fold in symmetry, too, over the draped *rebozo* as they hold a bouquet of flowers and a letter to her friend Trotsky. The carefully chosen colors reflect Kahlo's appreciation of beauty.

Borrowing from the Mexican folk art tradition, Kahlo chose a primitive, or naive, style for some of her paintings. She admired the primitive Mexican paintings, created by amateur artists, in which solid objects appear flat and their sizes are not in proportion.

Kahlo's natural curiosity about art had led her to read many art books. She had learned to draw and to model clay at the Prepatoria. Then she had improved her drawing skills by working for an engraver and commercial printer. Her artistic father and husband had encouraged her. It is no wonder that Kahlo's primitive-like paintings also showed advanced art techniques. Her uses of line, color, shape, form, texture, and space reflect her skillful understanding of design.

Even after Kahlo's style became more realistic

Frida Kahlo. **Self-Portrait Dedicated to Leon Trotsky.** *(Autorretrato dedicado a Leon Trotsky.) 1937. Oil on masonite. 30 x 24 inches. The National Museum of Women in the Arts, Gift of the Honorable Clare Boothe Luce.* Kahlo painted this self-portrait for her friend Leon Trotsky, who was exiled from the Soviet Union and lived with his wife in the Casa Azul for two years.

Frida Kahlo. **Self-Portrait (The Frame).** (*Autorretrato con marco integrado y dos pájaros.*) *c. 1938. Oil on aluminum and glass, 29 x 22 cm. Musée National d'Art Moderne, Centre Georges Pompidou, Paris.*
The Louvre (LOO-vr), a world-famous art museum in Paris, purchased this self-portrait from the Mexique exhibit held there in 1938.

than primitive, she continued to paint on a variety of surfaces — small pieces of copper, tin, aluminum, wood, cardboard, or glass. Like many artists, she also painted on canvas. She was a free spirit who followed few rules. In *Self-Portrait* (*The Frame*), she created a frame of bright flowers and birds.

In 1938, when Kahlo was thirty-one years old, she traveled to New York City for the first solo exhibition of her work. The exhibit appeared in the art gallery of Julien Levy, who had heard about some of Kahlo's paintings displayed in a Mexico City gallery.

Soon afterward she left for Paris to attend an art show, called Mexique, also featuring her paintings. A famous French poet, André Breton, organized the exhibit and claimed that Kahlo's powerfully delicate paintings were like "a ribbon around a bomb." He had founded a French artists group called the Surrealists, whose art appeared dreamlike yet real. Even though Kahlo's paintings were based on her real-life experiences, rather than on her dreams, they appear surrealistic.

When Frida returned home in 1939, Diego decided to file for divorce. Perhaps he was involved with someone else or felt upset by the close friendships Frida had formed apart from him. Whatever the reasons for the divorce were, it hurt Frida deeply. To cope with her feelings, she painted.

The Two Fridas, probably her best-known painting, shows both the Frida that Diego loved, wearing a Tehuana skirt and blouse, and the Frida he had rejected, who wears a white Victorian dress. Kahlo painted a turbulent sky and exposed hearts to symbolize pain from love. The unloved Frida's dress is torn, her heart broken, while the

other's heart is whole. The loved Frida holds a miniature portrait of Diego as a boy. From there a red vein leads the viewer's eye all the way to the surgical pincers of the rejected Frida. The magic flow of love to Diego — Frida's blood — drips onto the white dress.

In 1940 Kahlo journeyed to San Francisco for medical treatment from Dr. Eloesser. Because he was a family friend, the doctor also knew that Frida and Diego still loved each other. So he helped them get back together. On December 8, Diego's fifty-fourth birthday, Frida and he were married again. Unfortunately, the happiness she

Frida Kahlo. **The Two Fridas.** (*Las dos Fridas.*) *1939. Oil on canvas. 173.5 x 173 cm. Instituto Nacional de Bellas Artes, Museo de Arte Moderno. Reproduction authorized by the National Institute of Fine Arts and Literature.*
By portraying the two Fridas clasping hands in the middle of this double self-portrait, Kahlo protected herself from the pain she suffered.

felt was short-lived. Within several months, she was saddened when her father died of a heart attack.

Diego and I 1929–1944 shows Frida's urge to unite with her husband. She loved and needed him so much that in some ways she wanted to *be* Diego. In this portrait Frida painted herself and Diego as a single head divided into two halves. A necklace of leafless tree branches may represent their stormy marriage that produced no children.

Frida Kahlo. **Diego and I 1929–1944 II.** (*Retrato doble, Diego y yo 1929–1944 II.*) *1944. Oil on wood. 26.5 x 18.5 cm. Collection of Francisco Gonzalez Vazquez, Mexico. Reproduction authorized by the National Institute of Fine Arts and Literature.*
This unusual portrait of two faces joined as one shows Kahlo's desire to be united with her husband.

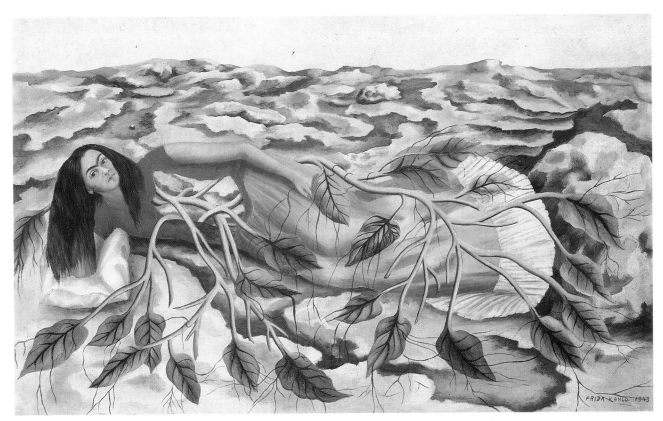

Frida Kahlo. **Roots.**
(*Raíces.*) 1943. Oil on metal.
30 x 50 cm. Private
collection.
Many of Kahlo's works are
considered Surrealist by art
critics. In *Roots*, Kahlo and
her surroundings appear
dreamlike yet real.

In her everyday life, Kahlo brought a sense of
dignity to her suffering. Instead of feeling sorry for
herself, she put up with things and tried to feel
happy. In most of her self-portraits, she looks
ahead with a steely strength that helped hide her
pain. Critics thought her themes were shocking,
but Kahlo did not care.

One such image, *Roots*, shows Kahlo lying on
the Pedregal, a region of volcanic rock in Mexico
where hardly any plants can grow. But Kahlo
painted a green vine thriving from a window in
her body. In this way she showed her feelings
about how her body and nature were one in the
same. The sprouting vine may represent her
unfulfilled wish to have children. Or perhaps it
symbolizes Kahlo's strong sense of being rooted in
the land and culture of Mexico.

Frida Kahlo with a Child.
The Bettmann Archive.
Even though Kahlo never
became a mother, she loved
to play with children.

Frida Kahlo. **Fulang-Chang
and Me.** *(Fulang-Chang y
yo.) 1937. Part one of
two-part ensemble (assembled
after 1939). Part one: 1937,
oil on composition board, 15¾
x 11 inches; painted mirror
frame (added after 1939),
22¼ x 17⅜ x 1¾ inches.
Part two (not shown): after
1939, mirror with painted
mirror frame, 25¼ x 19⅛ x
1¾ inches. Collection, The
Museum of Modern Art, New
York. Mary Sklar Bequest.
Photograph © 1992 The
Museum of Modern Art, New
York.*

Kahlo's paintings often showed her sense of humor as well. *In Fulang-Chang and Me,* the artist's full lips and dark, wide eyes resemble those of her pet monkey. Even the tips of her hair appear like the fur of Fulang-Chang. Throughout her life, Kahlo would feel an animal restlessness within herself, along with an uneasy tension about her marriage and her health.

Kahlo's lifelong struggle with her health became a symbol of the courage that has strengthened women when faced with pain and suffering. Her artwork shows the myth and magic of the Mexican culture, which often challenges death itself. Just as a *matador,* or bullfighter, dares the bull to charge his red cape, Kahlo teased away feelings of death through her art.

During the early 1940s, Kahlo's works were exhibited in several major art museums in the United States. Soon her reputation as an artist caught on in Mexico as well, and she received Mexican fellowships and commissions.

In 1942 Kahlo taught art classes to children at La Esmeralda, a public school for painting and sculpting in Mexico City. She taught her students to be self-critical. She gave her opinions of their artwork but made it clear that what she said was only a personal view. She taught them to draw and paint what was inside their houses — clay jars, popular art, furniture, and toys. She took the students into the streets, to the markets, slums, churches, nearby villages, and pyramids. They sang revolutionary Mexican songs and laughed together.

Bernard G. Silberstein.
**Frida Kahlo in Her
Bedroom.** *c. 1943.*
In 1953, from this same
bed, the weak yet cheerful
artist would greet her guests
at her first solo exhibit in
Mexico.

After a few months of teaching, Kahlo's lingering ailments from the long-ago bus accident prevented her from traveling into the city. So for several years her students traveled to the Casa Azul in Coyoacán to take lessons. They loved her so much that they came to be called "Los Fridos."

In 1950 Kahlo became so sick from spinal problems that she had to stay in a hospital in Mexico City for a year. She always showed a grand sense of humor and a love of life. From her hospital bed she produced puppet shows with her feet. Her room was filled with colorful Mexican decorations — candy skulls, a brightly painted candle holder shaped like a tree of life, and white doves made of wax with paper wings that reminded Kahlo of peace. Beside her bed she kept stacks of books, pots of paint, and brushes.

Kahlo's hospital visitors signed their names on her plaster body casts, which she decorated with feathers, mirrors, photographs, pebbles, and ink. Diego read poetry aloud or, pretending to be a circus bear, danced around her bed with a tambourine.

In 1953 Frida Kahlo was given her first solo exhibit in her native land. On the night of the opening, her health took a turn for the worse, however, and doctors forbade her to move. But that did not stop Kahlo. She asked that her four-poster bed be moved to the gallery. A police-escorted ambulance arrived at the exhibit. Kahlo was carried on a stretcher through the crowd of her friends and supporters. From her bed, she greeted fans all evening long. Always the center of attention, the bedridden artist became the source of energy in the gala exhibit opening.

Frida Kahlo. **Long Live Life.** (*Viva la vida.*) 1954. *Oil on masonite. 52 x 72 cm. Museo Frida Kahlo, Mexico City. Reproduction authorized by the National Institute of Fine Arts and Literature.* This final painting became Kahlo's farewell to life.

From her bed at the Casa Azul, Kahlo experimented with a new theme — still life. *Long Live Life* is Kahlo's last painting. Ripe red watermelons are sliced in many ways against a beautiful blue sky. Eight days before her death, Kahlo picked up a brush to apply her signature and her final salute to life.

On July 13, 1954, seven days after her forty-seventh birthday, Frida Kahlo died in her bed at the Casa Azul. When Diego heard the news, his face and body sank into deep sorrow. A great crowd came in the rain to pay respect to Kahlo's body, which was taken to lie in state at the Palace of Fine Arts in Mexico City until her cremation.

During her lifetime, Kahlo had only two solo shows, and her work was purchased mostly by friends. Today her work is exhibited around the world, and she is known as one of the greatest painters Mexico has ever produced. In 1984 the Mexican government decreed her art to be a national patrimony, among the heritage of male artists, including Diego.

Although Frida Kahlo is gone, we have her art to remember her by. It is a reminder of how a powerful artist overcame pain and sorrow by using her strengths and talents.